THE
ALCHEMISTS:
MAGIC
INTO
SCIENCE

To E. John DeWaard,
a renaissance man whose interest in the occult
is combined with a thorough knowledge of science

Thomas G. Aylesworth

THE ALCHE

MAGIC INTO SCIENCE

Addison-Wesley

MISTS

NoťAR

j 540.1
A
c. 2
N. L.

Addisonian Press titles
by Thomas G. Aylesworth

Servants of the Devil
Werewolves and Other Monsters
Vampires and Other Ghosts
The Alchemists: Magic Into Science

An Addisonian Press Book

Text Copyright © 1973
by Thomas G. Aylesworth
Illustrations Copyright © 1973
by Addison-Wesley Publishing Co., Inc.
All Rights Reserved
Addison-Wesley Publishing Company, Inc.
Reading, Massachusetts 01867
Printed in the United States of America
First Printing

Library of Congress Cataloging in Publication Data

Aylesworth, Thomas G.
   The alchemists.

   SUMMARY: Traces the history of alchemy and the
activities of the alchemists who developed the foundations
of modern science.
   "An Addisonian Press book."
   1. Alchemists—Biography—Juvenile literature.
2. Alchemy—Juvenile literature. [1. Alchemy.
2. Alchemists] I. Title.
QD24.A1A94   540'.1 [B]   72–7495
ISBN 0–201–00143–8

CONTENTS

An eighteenth century satirical cartoon of an alchemist, "The Marquis of Outrage-Nature in his Laboratory Dress."

INTRODUCTION / The history of alchemy is a history of men who were, on the one hand, scientists, and on the other hand, dreamers. There is no way to separate the practical chemistry of the alchemists from their occasional fanciful excursions into the unknown.

The early craftsmen who were able to mix a little bit of this with a drop or two of that and come up with startling new materials began to think of what they had done. Wouldn't it be possible, they may have said to themselves, to change common metals into gold or silver? And, if they could find a magic elixir, might they be able to prolong life?

These men were protected by the princes, kings, and popes of their day. Men of power, it would seem, always need more wealth. And more health.

Alchemy was a medieval, metallurgical, superstition-laden, chemical science with touches of sorcery, religion, and experimentation. But the alchemists laid down the groundwork for modern science.

The situation was complex. And in the ranks of the alchemists there were crooks, quacks, and frauds. But there were many honest scientists, too. This is their story—the story of how some men tried to turn magic into science.

Thomas G. Aylesworth
Stamford, Connecticut
1973

ONE / THREE MEN OF FAME / One of the most famous alchemists of all times may have been a man who never lived at all. Strange as this may sound, the history behind this individual is a story of its own. The man's name was Merlin. And he was a magician.

Supposedly, Merlin was the resident court wizard and prophet in the Court of King Arthur and the Knights of the Round Table. No one is quite sure whether or not Merlin ever existed. Actually, no one is sure whether King Arthur and his knights ever existed either.

If there was a Merlin, he was probably a seer named Myrddin, who lived in the sixth century, A.D. Reputed to be a trouble-maker of sorts, he caused the battle of Arderydd in the 570's between several British chieftains. As a punishment, a vision in the sky addled his mind and sent him wandering and raving prophesies through the Welsh and Scottish forests. It's very possible that the

Merlin could prophesy the future,
but, it was said,
he couldn't foresee his own fate.
Here the magician is being enchanted
by a damsel at King Arthur's court.

legend of Merlin the Magician grew from the stories of this man as they passed through generations of time.

The first report we hear of him in literature is in the work of Geoffrey of Monmouth, the English author in the twelfth century. Geoffrey published some prophesies and said that they were the words of a Merlin the Magician. It was only a matter of time until Merlin and King Arthur were linked together.

Now if Merlin ever met Arthur at all, it was when he was a young man and Arthur was an old man. But Geoffrey probably wanted to make his story more interesting so he used a Merlin who was the older of the two. Consequently, he shifted Merlin's birthday back to 450 A.D. When this falsehood was discovered it was explained that there might have been two Merlins. Some historians believe this was possible. If this was so, it is very likely that a so-called Merlin the Magician did exist. But who's to say for sure?

Now Geoffrey's legend gave Merlin a human mother and a demon father. He also gave him remarkable powers and the ability to see far into the future. According to the myth, Merlin was the cause of Arthur's birth. Merlin cast a spell on Uther, the king of Britain at the time, and caused him to look exactly like the Duke of Cornwall. The duke had imprisoned his beautiful wife, Igraine, in Tintagel Castle and Uther was able to enter the castle and rescue her. They fell in love and out of all this swash-buckling, Arthur was born.

Merlin went on helping Arthur. When Uther died, no one could figure out who should be the next king. So Merlin persuaded the Archbishop of Canterbury to gather all the British barons together in the city of London. Merlin had prepared a stone "in midst thereof was an anvil of steel a foot on high, and therin stuck a fair sword naked by the point, and letters there were written in gold about the sword that said thus: Whoso pulleth out the sword of this stone and anvil is rightwise king born of all England."

Needless to say, many young men tried to pull out the sword. But Merlin fixed it so only Arthur was able to lift the sword from the stone.

As the years went by, romantic authors began to credit Merlin with Arthur's education. They said that he helped to establish the Round Table and encouraged King Arthur to send the knights out after The Holy Grail—the cup that Jesus used at the Last Supper. They also told of a love affair with a strange girl, Nimue, who eventually locked Merlin in a cave, from which he was never able to escape.

In the nineteenth century, Merlin was thought to be a symbol of early science. And he has this kind of image in the *Idylls of the King,* a long poem by Tennyson.

By the time that T. H. White wrote his three volume history of King Arthur's Court, *The Once and Future King,* Merlin had acquired the ability to remember the future and forget the past. But this man belonged to an age in which science was in its infancy—a mixture of religion, magic, superstition, and experimentation. And, whether he existed or not, Merlin was a man who has been grouped with the early alchemists.

What is an alchemist? What did they do? To begin to answer these questions, perhaps we ought to take a look at two. One of them was an honest seeker after the truth and the other was a rogue. The first is Paracelsus and the second is Cagliostro.

Paracelsus was a wanderer who could not get along with his fellow man. Biochemist, surgeon, physician, magician, and alchemist—this was Paracelsus. He was one of the first men to take the folklore and witchcraft of the past and use it in modern medical science. And in searching for the truth, he was ridiculed, taunted, and exiled. He was a man who said: "Medicine is not merely a science but an art. It does not consist in compounding pills and plasters and drugs of all kinds, but it deals with the processes of life . . . The character of the physician may act more powerfully upon the patient than all the drugs employed."

This Swiss alchemist was born near Zurich in 1493. Although he usually used the name Paracelsus, it is said that his complete name was Philippus Aureolus Theophrastus Paracelsus Bombastus von Hohenheim.

Paracelsus was taught—largely by his father—to become a physician, and there is little evidence that he ever attended any university, although some people believe that he took courses at the University in Basel, Switzerland, during his sixteenth year. This lack of education is not surprising because medicine was not a popular course of study at universities at that time.

So, early in his career, Paracelsus decided to toss away all the books of medicine and learn his art from nature itself. He traveled all over from 1513 to 1524, studying metals, chemistry, and medicine. He was brought before many of the rulers of the world—kings in Europe as well as India, Egypt, and Arabia. Finally, he returned to Switzerland to settle down in the town of Basel, which at that time, was a favorite spot for learned men from all over Europe.

He was appointed to the chair of medicine at the university but he did not seem to fit in. He rejected the

PARACELSUS.

Paracelsus believed that
man consisted of three
elements: salt represented
the body, sulfur the soul,
and mercury the spirit.
He thought he could
rearrange the amounts of the
elements to change man.

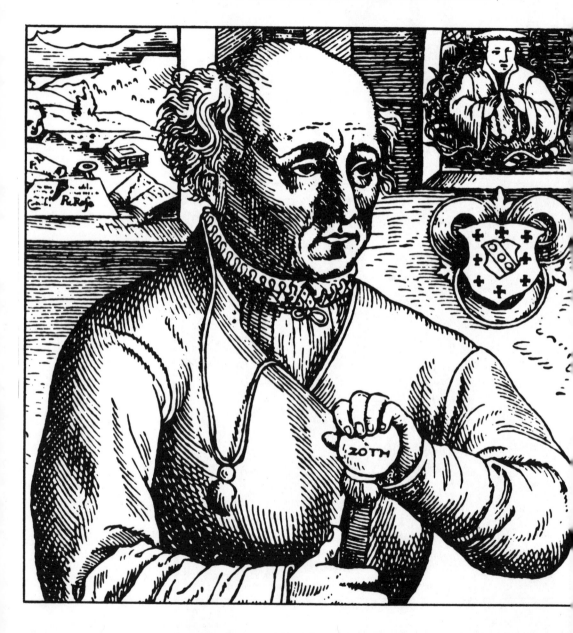

Stories of forming little
human beings—a *homunculus*—with such formulas
as Paracelsus'—might have
inspired the writer of *Frankenstein*
and the developers of modern robots.

medical teachings of the ancient physician, Galen, (whose ideas were almost sacred) and burned, not only Galen's medical books, but also those of Avicenna, another respected alchemist.

Was he in trouble with his fellow professors!

He turned his back on the medical establishment, and he also had the nerve to lecture to his classes in German, which they understood, rather than in Latin, with which they had trouble.

The medical profession waged an unending war against this man. The physicians of the time were so conservative that they could never forgive him because of three things. First, he would not admit that there were any cures superior to his—other than nature. Second, he invented his own medicines, turning his back on the superstitious remedies of the medical profession of the time. Third, and probably the worst, he cured his patients with his new-fangled methods.

This great physician was a different sort of man. To begin with, he tested many natural substances to see if they might be used in the healing art. And most amazing of all, Paracelsus did not seem to be too interested in what many called the philosopher's stone.

One of the things that alchemists were constantly looking for was the philosopher's stone. This was a substance that would somehow change base metals, such as mercury or lead, into gold. Paracelsus once wrote: "Many have discussed alchemy claiming gold and silver can be made by it. We hold this not to be very important. We deem important only the preparation of effective medicines . . . yes, this is important—produce arcana (mysterious knowledge) and use them against all diseases." But there were people who believed that Paracelsus had discovered the philosopher's stone anyway, when he was only 28 years old.

Nevertheless, in his experiments, Paracelsus seemed to lean heavily on the testing of metals—possibly because he had learned so much metallurgy from his father. He was not above getting some information about folk medicine from "barbers, midwives, sorcerers, alchemists, in monasteries, among common people and nobles, from the wise, and from the simple-minded."

He had an unusual view of alchemy. He believed that God had created the earth and that everything that man needed could be found somewhere. So, in one way or another, every man was an alchemist. A baker making bread was an alchemist—he had found the secrets of wheat and yeast. Of course there were other secrets of nature that had not been discovered yet. And it was the job of alchemists with scientific dispositions to find them out. Nature had a remedy for every disease, but man had not discovered them all yet.

Paracelsus also described the "sap of life" (blood circulation) more than 100 years before William Harvey discovered it. He invented a new type of smelling salts, a very effective sleeping potion, and developed a blood purifier that was rich in iron. Not only these, but he also discovered *laudanum*, an opium compound, and was the first physician to use it to kill pain, and the first man to use mercury in the treatment of venereal disease.

Another object the alchemists searched for was the *homunculus*. This was the product of the laboratory—an artificially created little man made of various substances who came alive according to a formula. Of course there never was any homunculus, just as there never was any philosopher's stone, but it represented an early search into the chemistry of developing a human life.

It is said that Paracelsus laid down a formula for making a homunculus. A man's sperm must be put into an air-tight jar. Then it must be buried in horse manure for

Cagliostro was an old-fashioned version
of a shyster, and in the eighteenth century
he fled from country to country to escape
the wrath of his victims . . . until . . .

forty days, and magnetized. Supposedly, during this time, the little man will begin to live and move, until by the end of the forty days it may resemble a man, but it will be transparent.

Now you must begin feeding the homunculus with human blood and keep it at the constant temperature of a mare's womb for forty weeks. At the end of this time, it will look like a perfect human child, except that it will be much smaller.

Paracelsus, who may or may not have believed in this recipe, then said: "It may be raised and educated like any other child until it grows older and is able to look after itself."

So much for the honest alchemist.

The biggest crook of them all was undoubtedly the Sicilian bandit Giuseppe Balsamo, who called himself Cagliostro. He was born in 1743 to a bankrupt store-keeper and his wife. He did have a royal godmother, the Countess Cagliostro, although this fact didn't seem to help his career a great deal.

As the boy grew up, it was obvious that he had some talents. Among these were running away from school, cheating storekeepers, and forging legal documents. He was jailed so many times for these activities that he decided to leave Palermo forever.

On his way across Sicily, he stopped for a time at Messina, where he learned the basic ideas of alchemy from a Greek scholar. Wherever he went, Cagliostro claimed that he did not know where he was born or who his parents were. Often he said that he had passed his childhood in Arabia and had lived in a palace. He also said that he had had a tutor and was provided with three slaves. The tutor was the one who started him off in the study of alchemy. He certainly made up good stories!

After a few months with the Greek scholar Cagliostro went to Rome, married, and engaged in the artistic endeavor of painting picture postcards.

Things weren't going too well at the studio, so he spent some time forging a commission for himself as a Major Balsamo in the Prussian Army. In the meantime, his creditors began knocking on his door, so he left Rome and began to pose as an army officer. But his hoax was discovered and he was thrown in jail.

When he got out, he and his wife started a trip to Spain. When they reached Madrid, their money ran out. So they left the Latin countries and headed for London in 1772.

About all that Balsamo earned in that first year in England was 100 pounds that he stole from an English physician. He took the money and, with a fellow Italian named Vivona, tried to set up an alchemic laboratory. His partner ran off with the money, and back Balsamo went to jail, this time to a debtors' prison.

But his wife found a wealthy patron who got Balsamo out of jail, moved both of the Cagliostros into his mansion, and gave them the run of the house. Balsamo, true to himself, got into trouble again. He was caught making advances to the daughter of the house, and he and his wife were thrown out into the street.

So he went to Paris to work as an alchemist. He claimed to have changed base metals into gold, and was able to bilk two wealthy Frenchmen out of a great deal of money. Then he disappeared. Only later did the Frenchmen learn that they were the victims of a sleight-of-hand trick, but by then it was too late.

For a while, Balsamo found it impossible to get any more wealthy sponsors, so finally he returned to Palermo in rags. But the police were waiting for him because of his past crimes. He was exiled from the city after he promised never to return again.

Next Balsamo decided to go into business for himself. So he became a traveling salesman of alchemic cosmetics. Off he went with his wife, first to the Island of Malta where he was received and befriended by the Grand Master of the Knights of Malta.

From Malta, they went to Naples, where they fell in with a rich merchant and moved into his house with him. Actually, the Balsamos were so content there that Mrs. Balsamo's father and brother were invited to come from Sicily, move in, and join the party. Eventually the merchant became a little fed up and so the Balsamos and the brother teamed up and went off to France. Apparently the father remained in Naples.

When the trio reached Marseilles, they found a rich Italian lady who was promised by Balsamo that he would make her young forever with the elixir of life, a magical substance that could prolong life. Naturally, he charged her a great deal of money for this little favor. After several months, she began to be suspicious that the alchemist would never let her see his philosopher's stone or his elixir of life. But he convinced her that he would need a little bit of time to travel around looking for chemicals. She was gullible enough to loan him money, as well as a coach and horses; so off the terrible three went, never to return.

The next time this rogue appeared it was as Colonel Cagliostro, the great alchemist, in Cadiz, Spain. Here he made the mistake of stealing a young nobleman's watch, and was arrested. He talked the nobleman out of pressing charges, but decided that he had better leave Spain, anyway. It was at this time that he and his brother-in-law parted company, each of them accusing the other of theft. Perhaps they both were right.

So Cagliostro and his wife set sail once again for England. On the way, a wonderful thing happened. Colonel Cagliostro became the famous Count Cagliostro.

The count and his wife docked in the year 1776. In London he became popular mostly because he had studied numerology and seemed to be able to give out good tips on the lottery. He was the darling of London society and was apparently able to talk everyone out of some cash as a down payment on a piece of the philosopher's stone. He claimed that he could make gold, he gave alms to the poor, and he practiced medicine.

But once again the gullible got wise, and he was forced to leave England. The Cagliostros then surfaced in the Netherlands. It was at The Hague that he announced that he had been the founder of a group of mystics who practiced "Egyptian Masonry." The Egyptian Rite, it was said, involved hypnotizing a child and causing him to see visions and make prophesies. Then spirits were conjured up, and supposedly one time they were able to raise the Archangel Michael. Cagliostro was able to take in a few members at exorbitant initiation fees, and then he ran off to Brussels.

There he found another sideline—the mixing of quack drugs. He had an Egyptian wine (just add spices to ordinary wine), refreshing pills (chicory, endive, and lettuce), and several other mixtures. He made enough money from these frauds to finance his next journey—to Jelgava, Latvia, where he tried several new kinds of tricks. There were spiritualistic seances complete with fake spirits from the grave. He received money from many merchants after promising them that he was going to build a factory that would magically turn hemp into silk. As soon as he got the money, he left Jelgava and went to Russia and then on to Poland.

In Warsaw, the Cagliostros obtained some money from a count by promising him that they would conjure up a special demon who would be the count's slave. The count eventually caught on and the Cagliostros were forced to flee to Frankfort, Germany. In every country they took advantage of anyone they could find. This time they found a few more members for their Egyptian Masonry group. They talked the initiates into financing the money to build a country estate to be used as a Lodge Hall. Needless to say, the 20,000 francs and the Cagliostros disappeared and the house was never built.

Finally the count found another sponsor. He was Cardinal de Rohan, who took him to France. When they got to Lyons, the Cagliostros set up a parent lodge of

"Freemasonry According to Egyptian Ritual." Naturally, he collected money from the new members.

But it was Paris that took him to heart. He became so popular in Parisian society that artists created busts of him to sell to wealthy Frenchmen. Painters decorated fans, snuff boxes, rings, coffee cups, and tea cups with the face of the famous "count." Even the poor people could afford his likeness—bakers made cookies shaped like his silhouette. All this for a man who merely said that he could make gold.

But it wasn't long before Cagliostro was once again in trouble. And this time it may not have been his fault. The Cardinal fell behind on his payments for a loan he had received. When he was arrested, the French police thought that they might as well take in Cagliostro since he was such a good friend of the Cardinal. This time, Cagliostro was acquitted, but the king ordered that he be sent out of France.

As Cagliostro left prison to be taken to the dock where he was to set sail for London, a procession of more than 5000 people went with him from Paris to the port of Boulogne. They knelt on the shore as the ship sailed off for England.

When he arrived in London, Cagliostro was extremely angry about the Paris episode so he issued a statement predicting that the French government would be overthrown. But the people in London had long memories. They remembered him only as a thief and a bandit, not as a prophet. So they asked him to leave the city. Soon Cagliostro found out that the people of other cities remembered him, too. Actually, there was hardly a large city in which he could show his face. Even some smaller towns would have nothing to do with him.

Almost without a penny in his pocket, he arrived back in Rome in 1789. He was all set to resume his alchemy practice when his prediction about the French crown came true. His success in prophesying went to his head. He began to go around uttering other predictions, some of them not to the liking of the Italian aristocracy. So he and his wife were thrown in jail again and what is worse, he was condemned to death as a heretic.

Pope Pius VI changed Cagliostro's death sentence to life imprisonment and Mrs. Cagliostro was sent to a convent. After the French government had changed hands, those same Frenchmen who had followed him to Boulogne sent an army to Italy to free him from his dungeon. But they arrived too late. Count Cagliostro had died. Some said that he was strangled in his cell by his jailer.

Yes, there were honest alchemists and frauds, foolish men and charlatans. Now let's take a look at how the whole thing began.

TWO / IN THE BEGINNING / Gold! Through-
out our history this metal has held a fascination for man.
Remember King Midas? Remember Rumpelstiltskin?
Remember the golden apple and the golden fleece? Did
you know that a golden bead worn on a necklace has
been thought to prevent all diseases? Or that British
sailors in the past wore golden earrings as protection
against drowning?

The story of gold goes back more than 5000 years,
when, it is said, the metal was first discovered in the
ancient land of Nubia, even before the time of the Egyptian pharaohs. Nubia was a territory along the Nile,
which later became a part of ancient Egypt and is now
part of the Sudan.

Right away, the ancient Nubians thought that gold was
holy. They believed that it was the sun brought down to

This alchemic woodcut
shows the Sun (gold) and the
Moon (silver) linked by a dragon (mercury).

earth. Their religion taught them that the sun was a god, and so gold must be part of a god.

Later, when Nubia was a part of ancient Egypt, this idea of the holiness of gold was upheld by the pharaoh. He and his followers thought that the ruler of Egypt was a god, too. So he could keep the gold for himself. After all, it was a part of the family, wasn't it? And taking all the gold is much easier than collecting a lot of taxes.

Things went along quietly for about 3000 years, and then came a Greek philosopher named Democritus. He announced a theory of atomic structure which stated that all matter on earth is composed of atoms. And these atoms are really tiny particles that cannot be divided. No one paid any attention to this theory for almost 25 centuries, until our modern atomic theory was developed.

No one paid attention, that is, except a philosopher who was living in the Egyptian city of Alexandria at about 200 B.C.E. He was also Greek, and he took such a fancy to the writings of Democritus that he even stole his name.

This new Democritus announced that he had "a stone that is no stone but that carries within it the seeds of the two precious metals (gold and silver) and is therefore capable of reproducing them." This is the first mention of the mythical tool of the alchemist—the philosopher's stone—a magic substance that would turn cheap materials into gold.

When later alchemists described the philosopher's stone, a lot of confusion occurred. It might be a stone, or merely a mixture of fire and water. It was called "a stone that is not a stone," or something that comes "from God but not from God." Perhaps it was made from animal, vegetable, and mineral substances, yet grew from flesh and blood. It was "unknown yet known to everybody." It was "worthless yet supremely valuable." Some considered it to be bean-shaped, reddish in color, and capable of giving off flashes of light, even in complete darkness. Who could follow these descriptions?

Democritus was the first alchemist—the first man, at least, to write about this mystical tool. He was also the first person to really explore the ancient science of alchemy. For he was one of the few people who believed that gold could be made from other materials. He collected formulas from metal workers, dyers, and glass blowers. His book, *Physica et Mystica,* was mostly a collection of them. Democritus was convinced that he could create a new material whenever a substance or substances were heated and changed color. Whether or not he had really discovered something new or perhaps gold was unimportant to many individuals. The possibility was enough to intrigue people. The study of the science of alchemy had begun.

A question might be asked here as to whether alchemy is a science or an art. There probably is no clear answer to the question. One person has defined it as "the science of the allegedly existing art of making gold." In other words, it is partly a science because it involves experimentation in a laboratory. Yet it can also be considered an art because it involves self-improvement and spiritual searches. This will become clearer as we get deeper into the subject.

In a very short time, the science had progressed to a lively occupation. An Egyptian named Zosimus published an alchemic encyclopedia of 28 volumes. This was about seven hundred years after the time of Democritus.

There were quite a few mistakes in this work. For example, Zosimus called the poison, arsenic, "the second mercury." He also thought that if he combined this second mercury in a certain way with copper, he could create silver.

Nevertheless, Zosimus was not a fool. He experimented. Some authorities credit him with the discovery

of lead acetate, a substance which we use today in dying, in varnish, and in certain types of medicine.

It was not long before men such as Zosimus acquired reputations which made them famous and eagerly sought after by many. In a short period of time alchemists realized that they had to protect themselves from becoming exploited by three different groups of people. And they were able to accomplish this by writing in their own language. This way no one other than a fellow alchemist could understand them.

So the alchemists used a number of symbols which had hidden meanings—the dragon, the king, the king's son, the gray wolf, the black crow, the lepers, the lion, the unicorn, the slaughter of the innocents, the royal marriage,

The two-headed dragon symbolized mercury.
It has two heads because mercury
can be either a metal or a liquid.

the tree, the peacock, and many more. All of these were
used so that their work would be kept secret.

The rulers of the day were one group of potential
enemies. It was not uncommon for a local king to im-
prison an alchemist and try to force him to reveal his
secrets. A few prisoners became wise and gave mysterious formulas to the king in order to appease him. Frequently, the kings' own soothsayers had a difficult time
translating the alchemist's instructions, but most everyone was content believing they had the secret of turning
lead into gold even if they didn't know how it was done.

Some rulers persecuted the alchemists in other ways.
In the fourth century, A.D., just after the time of Zosimus,
the Roman emperor Diocletian ordered a search to be

made throughout all Egypt for alchemic writings. These manuscripts were then to be burned.

The leaders of the church were another group of people that did not trust the alchemists. They believed alchemists were exploring an area very close to heresy. The followers of this science, said the churchmen, not only tried to change metals into gold and silver, but they also tried to create and perfect human nature. And they tried to do this by appealing to God through the chemistry and mystery of alchemy. This went against the teachings of the powerful church at the time. The religious leaders believed that man got closer to God through the faith of conventional religion. Becoming a better person was achieved, they probably thought, through piety and pure thoughts, not by chemical magic.

So the alchemist tried to get around the opposition of the church by creating a Biblical legend about his art. Borrowing heavily from the book of Genesis in the Bible, he said alchemy was brought down from Heaven by angels. He also claimed that Noah was an alchemist and had preserved his techniques and mysteries during the flood. It was even said that Noah was spared by God because he had kept the alchemic secrets. Even so, it is doubtful whether the church believed this theory.

The third group which worried the alchemist was also the most numerous—the greedy people of the world. In

the fifteenth century, Thomas Norton wrote a poem that
explains this feeling:

This art must ever secret be,
The cause whereof is this, as ye may see;
If one evil man had thereof all his will,
All Christian peace he might easily spill,
And with his pride he might pull down
Rightful kings and princes of renown.

Another early alchemist also wrote about the greedy
souls on earth: "I disdain, loathe, and detest the idolizing
of silver and gold by which the pomps and vanities of the
world are celebrated. Ah! filthy, evil, ah! vain nothing-
ness."

During the second and third centuries, A.D., many of
the alchemists were afraid of the church and secretly
worshipped the ancient Greek god, Hermes Trismegistus
—the god of learning. Even today, alchemy is sometimes
referred to as the Hermetic Science. But by the end of the
third century, alchemists had made their peace with the
church. And the science was now at last free to flourish.

Let us take a look at the city of Alexandria, the center of
Egyptian learning, early in the Christian Era. There was
a very popular industry in this area. It was the business
of making cheap imitations of expensive products, and
selling them to poor people. Simulated pearls, dyes that

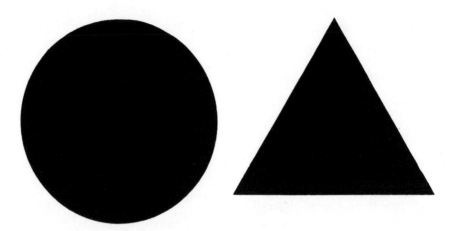

The symbols of the four elements of the ancient world had various meanings—the circle (air), the triangle (fire), the square (earth), and the crescent (water).

looked like royal purple, metal mixtures that looked like silver and gold were made. Naturally, some people didn't want imitations. What then would be more natural than for some ingenious individual to try and reproduce the real thing, but cheaply? So the Alexandrian alchemist tried to make his own gold and silver.

Very often he would melt tin, lead, copper, or iron. When the metals were in liquid form he would add mercury, arsenic, or antimony to give the end result a white appearance. This made it look like silver. Or perhaps he would add something else which would turn the material the color of gold. He was not really interested in the physical properties or the chemical reactions of the metal —just its color. At first it was believed that five of the seven base metals—lead, copper, tin, iron, mercury— could be changed into the other two, gold or silver. These men believed in the old theory of Aristotle—that the world is made up of four elements, earth, air, fire, and water, either in their pure states or in a combination. And there are four conditions in which these elements can be found—moist, dry, hot, or cold. Fire is hot and dry. Earth is dry and cold. Water is cold and moist. Air is moist and hot.

Next the alchemist assigned a heavenly body to each one of the seven base metals. This was supposed to exert a sort of astrological power over them. The ruler of gold

This woodcut depicts
the joining of gold and silver.
The Sun and the man represent gold;
the Moon and woman represent silver.

was, of course, the sun; silver had the moon; mercury had Mercury; copper had Venus; iron had Mars; tin had Jupiter; and lead had Saturn.

Lead, that dark and heavy metal, was thought by the alchemists to occupy the lowest rung on the metallic ladder. They gave it Saturn as its symbol, because that planet was the farthest distant heavenly body that could be seen with the naked eye. Some alchemists believed that since lead was the most imperfect metal, it must be the one to start with when they attempted to make gold. So lead must first be changed to tin, then tin must be changed to iron, iron to copper, copper to mercury, mercury to silver, and finally silver to gold.

Hans Biedermann, a science historian, said: "The alchemists moved along two tracks, which to most of us will never meet—one mystical and the other chemical. But to the adepts these were one track, for they believed that

through the processes of the art they could both perfect themselves as human beings and perfect metals by turning them into gold."

Alchemy is usually described as a false science. Sometimes it is said that it was based on a search for a method of making gold. Some people say that it was the forerunner of modern chemistry. But this is not the whole truth. The alchemist was as much interested in transforming humans into more perfect beings as he was in changing lead or mercury to gold. This is what most historians forget.

Actually, the alchemists believed that, just as in their experiments in search of gold, the human being could be made perfect. The first step in changing metal to gold was to heat the base metal. Just as the first step in attaining human perfection should be the death of a person's evil personality. The fire of alchemy then symbolized the period of self-searching and self-doubt which any penitent must go through. Then, as the material becomes gold, so too does the human being achieve perfection. Unfortunately, just as the alchemist never found gold, neither did he achieve human perfection. But he tried.

Early in the Christian Era, the alchemists, improving on Aristotle, developed the idea that all metals are composed of sulfur and mercury. Sulfur is related to fire, gold, and the sun. Mercury is related to water, silver, and the moon. Sulfur is male; mercury is female. The next step was to search for a way to combine the two metals. Out of this combination would come the philosopher's stone. (Remember Democritus announced that he had found such an object back in 200 B.C.E.)

How did they go about trying to make precious metals? Several steps had to be taken and most of these steps worked best when they were performed under a certain sign of the zodiac.

The first step was called the *calcinatio*. This is a fancy term for the burning of a substance in an open flame. Alchemists used this process to change a metal or some other solid substance into a powder, and it was described as turning the metal into chalk. *Putrefactio* was the second step. This stands for decay or rotting. Next came *sublematio*, or evaporation.

The process of *solutio* followed. The alchemists did not necessarily think of this as the mixing of a dry substance with a wet one to form a solution. Sometimes they merely meant that they wanted to make a liquid by smelting or melting it.

The fifth stage was the *distillatio*. In the beginning, this meant the same thing as the distillation process we know today. A liquid is heated, vapors come off, and they are cooled to form a solid. But later, the alchemists included the removal of a liquid by means of a wick or a

To make gold,
alchemists used furnaces for
the evaporation stage of the process.

And this evaporation step was most effective
when performed under the zodiac sign of Libra;
its symbol was a flock of birds.

siphon. When the mixture finally cools and solidifies or crystallizes, this was called *coagulatio*. And the final step was *extractio* which the alchemists hoped would produce the actual gold.

There were other minor steps that could be thrown into the whole process. *Congelatio, fixatio, projectio, multiplicatio,* and several more. But the seven mentioned above were the most important. The question is one of technique. How did they do these things? The answer is a disappointing one. The alchemists were so secretive that we are not sure.

At any rate, here is a description of a transmutation that was supposed to have occurred in the seventeenth century:

"Among many transformations performed by the same powder [supposedly the philosopher's stone] was one by the Elector of Mayence, in 1651. He made projections with all the precautions possible to a learned and skillful philosopher. The powder enclosed in gum tragacanth [a substance made from an Asiatic herb] to retain it effectually, was put into the wax of a taper [candle], which was lighted, the wax being then placed at the bottom of a crucible. These preparations were undertaken by the Elector himself. He poured four ounces of quicksilver [mercury] on the wax, and put the whole into a fire covered with charcoal above, below and around. Then they began blowing to the utmost, and in about half an hour on removing the coals, they saw that the melted gold was overred, the proper colour being green. The baron said the matter was yet too high and it was necessary to put some silver into it. The Elector took some coins out of his pocket, put them into the melting pot, combined the liquified silver with the matter in the crucible [pot], and having poured out the whole when in perfect fusion into an ingot [mold], he found after cooling, that it was very fine gold, but rather hard, which was attributed to the ingot. On again melting, it became exceedingly soft and the Master of the Mint declared to His Highness that it was more than twenty-four carats and that he had never seen so fine a quality of the precious metal."

Although that passage seems to lack some concrete directions for making gold, let's pursue the subject and follow a few more of these early alchemists.

Geber was not able to make gold, for he was unsuccessful in discovering the philosopher's stone.

THREE / THE PERSIANS /

There is a good deal that we do not know about a man called Geber. We think that he was born sometime between 721 and 730 A.D. He died somewhere between 810 and 815. We are not sure what to call him, either. Geber was not his real name; it was what Latin-speaking people called him, since his correct name, Abu Musa Jabir ibn Hayyan, was so complicated.

He was also sometimes called Al-Azid, because he belonged to a South Arabian tribe, or Al-Kufi, Al-Tusi, and Al-Sufi. But let's call him Geber.

We think that Geber was the court chemist to caliph Harun al-Rashid (a famous Mohammedan ruler from *The Arabian Nights*). While Geber was at court, he claimed that he wrote a few books—500 of them on philosophy, 1300 on machinery, 1300 on art, 500 on medicine, plus books on magic, spells, exorcism, astrology, and astronomy. That is a little hard to believe.

According to modern folklore, Harun al-Rashid was supposed to have been a kind, wise, and just leader. But he really was a tyrant. Geber had been appointed to the court by the caliph's advisors. Later he was lucky to have escaped with his life. Harun al-Rashid had his chief advisor impaled and chased the rest of them out of the country. Apparently their leader was a very moody individual.

The only things that we know about Geber are some of his scientific beliefs and discoveries. He was the first person to have the idea that all metals were composed of sulfur and mercury. Sulfur, he said, contained the hot and dry elements in their purest state, and mercury contained the elements of coldness and wetness. When these were not pure, or were not combined in the proper proportions, we saw them as silver, lead, tin, iron, copper, or mercury. But when they were pure and combined in the proper proportions, we had gold.

Mercury was the element of motion, according to Geber, and so it must have been a part of the philosopher's stone. And the closer a substance came to the mobility of mercury, the closer it was to being changed into gold. Sulfur was the element that made things burn. Nothing, indeed, would burn unless it had some sulfur in it. So obviously, all substances that could be chemically experimented with contained both of these metals.

If they did not have sulfur, they would not burn. And if they did not contain mercury, they would not melt.

The problem of making gold, according to Geber, was that truly pure sulfur and mercury were almost never to be found. If they were found, anyone could manufacture all of the gold that he wanted. That was a pretty transparent excuse for not making gold, but there were chemists who believed it right up to the seventeenth century.

Geber's ideas about needing both sulfur and mercury to make gold were revolutionary. Before he came along, chemists had been throwing things together in a haphazard fashion. Here is an ancient formula from a sanskrit magic text:

Twenty parts of platinum
Twenty parts of silver
Two hundred forty parts of brass
One hundred twenty parts of nickel
Melt each separately in different crucibles and then combine. Gold will result.

Geber's book, *The Book of Rules*, listed recipes for making many chemicals which are commonly used today: sal ammoniac (ammonium chloride, a white salt often used in dry cell batteries today), white lead (the basic substance of lead paint), nitric acid (a basic chemical used in manufacturing fertilizers, plastics, and hundreds of

Some alchemic
laboratories
were in a
constant state
of confusion.

other products), acetic acid (used in the making of vinegar, plastics, and some insecticides), and various properties of glass, and even steel.

Geber could estimate the copper content of a metal by looking at the greenish color of the flame when the metal was heated. He experimented with the dying of various materials and came up with a system of waterproofing cloth and leather and he developed a luminous ink and a rust inhibitor. But alas, he was never able to make gold.

Geber looked everywhere for his materials. He used not only metals and salts, but also bones, blood, lion's hair and urine, vipers, foxes, cattle, gazelles, donkeys, olives, jasmine, onions, ginger, pepper, mustard, and pears.

Geber, like so many other alchemists, failed at his main task—finding the philosopher's stone. But look at what he accomplished.

Another Persian came along after Geber. He was Rhazes (or Rhasis, or Rasi Mohammed Ebn-Secharjah Aboubekr Arrasi, or Abu-Bekr Mohammed ibn Zakariyya ar-Razi), who was born in the Persian city of Rayy, probably about 825 A.D. He died at the ripe old age of 100 or thereabouts.

In the beginning, Rhazes looked as though he might turn out to be a professional student. He studied philosophy, poetry, and music in his home town until he was about 30 years old. Then he decided to go off to Baghdad to study medicine.

Rhazes was reported to have a good heart. He devoted his healing art to helping the poor. He built a hospital in Baghdad and another in his home town. In addition to treating the sick he also became interested in alchemy.

It is said that he wrote 226 science books. Unfortunately one of them on changing metal into gold got him in trouble. The book was presented to the Emir Almansour, Prince of Khorassan. The prince was so delighted that he gave Rhazes 1000 pieces of gold on the condition that he could observe some of the alchemist's experiments.

A laboratory was set up for Rhazes. But you can guess the result. The experiments were failures. The prince was so angry that it is said he took Rhazes' book and beat him with the volume.

You can choose your own ending. Some say the alchemist died as a result of this beating. Others say the beating caused Rhazes to go blind and he died later in extreme poverty. But he had led a full life. And his writings were still being used as textbooks in Europe as late as the seventeenth century.

Rhazes, however, went the other alchemists one better. Not only did he believe that gold could be made from metals, but he also believed that quartz and glass could be made into diamonds, rubies, and other precious stones.

This type of container was often used by alchemists to store mercury.

A seventeenth century German engraving of some pieces of laboratory apparatus used by alchemists

Rhazes was probably the first alchemist to devote himself to laboratory work. It is said that his laboratory was one of the first to contain beakers, flasks, vials, basins, pitchers, slides, melting pots, candles, oil lamps, forges, ovens, crucibles, spatulas, hammers, sand baths, steam boilers, cloth filters, retorts, funnels, mortars, and pestles. Many of these can be found today in almost any chemistry laboratory.

What did he discover? Some of it was pretty silly. His treatment for insomnia consisted of boiling the left eye of a porcupine in oil. Then he would drop the mixture into the patient's ear (which one was not specified), and supposedly the patient would fall asleep immediately.

Just so we don't waste the right eye of the poor porcupine, we can boil it first. Then mix it with other ingredients and use it as an eyewash. This will enable the user to see in the dark.

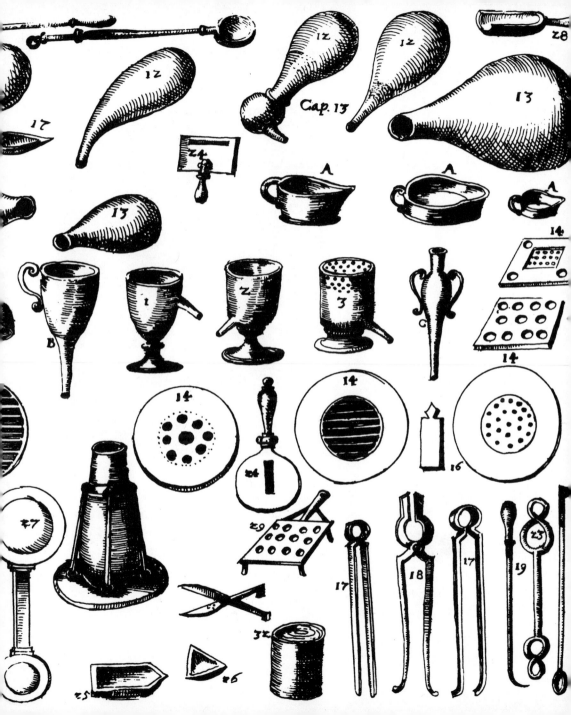

Avicenna was unusual,
for he did not believe
in the philosopher's stone.

Perhaps a married couple was experiencing difficulty having children. This condition could be remedied by having the man and wife eat toads.

Quite a few people believed the medicines worked. This leads many to conclude that the success of Rhazes' treatments depended on the cooperation of the patient.

In other words, much was accomplished by the power of suggestion.

Then along came Avicenna—"The Arabian Aristotle," "The Prince Among Physicians." He was born in 980 in Russia. His full name was abu-Ali al-Husain ibn Abdullah ibn-Sina but some say that his real name was Al-Sheikh Al-Rayis Abu Ali Al-Hossein ben Abdallah ben Sina. No wonder they called him Avicenna.

Avicenna was an exceptional student of many subjects. But he switched to medicine and was made a physician at the age of 17.

Avicenna was not a true alchemist, for he did not believe that gold could be created from base metals. Base metals, he thought, were not pure enough to be changed into gold. Therefore he did not believe in the philosopher's stone either. What he did believe in, although he never found it, was the existence of an elixir—a counterpart to the philosopher's stone. Specifically, an elixir was a remedy for all human physical ills. This belief set him apart from previous alchemists and from here on alchemic experiments entered a new era. For the discovery of such a substance would lead to everlasting life and health on earth. Sometimes called the Grand Arcanum, the elixir of life, along with the philosopher's stone, was to become the dream of the alchemists who followed Avicenna.

FOUR / ALCHEMY MOVES WEST /

The man who was most responsible for the spread of alchemy throughout the Western World was Albert von Bollstaedt, better known as Albertus Magnus. There are those who say that he was the inventor of the pistol and the cannon, but we can discount that. The point is that he was a respected priest, scholar, technician, and alchemist. And more than 600 years after he died, in 1931, he was canonized as a Saint of the Roman Catholic Church.

Albertus was born in 1193 in Lauingen, Germany. Like so many geniuses (Thomas Aquinas, Thomas Edison, and Albert Einstein, to name only three), he was considered to be stupid when he was a youngster. But he was religious, and he claimed that he had had a visitation from the Virgin Mary one night, and she granted him a wish—to be more intelligent.

Albertus Magnus was a believer in both science and magic. ▶

MAGNVS · ALBERTVS BOLSTADIVS COGNOMENTO

Mitra pedumq. oneri tibi quondam Alberte, fuerunt.
Dulcius est Sophiæ delituiſſe ſinu

There was no doubt that his intellect had blossomed, and, because of his vision, no one was surprised when he decided to enter the Dominican Order of Priests. He was sent to teach at various German monasteries. He taught at the University of Paris, was made a bishop in a town in Bavaria, and retired to become a professor in Cologne.

His reputation as a scientist was widespread, and it may have been embarrassing. For example, one story tells of his inviting some guests to his house in the middle of winter. The guests were surprised when Albertus informed them that they were to eat outdoors—in the snow. Some of them were insulted, but Albertus had them sit down, and behold! The snow around them melted away, the sun shone brightly, the birds sang, and it was summer. That story is impossible to believe, but it does show how much people thought of Albertus's power.

Albertus was called *the doctor universalis,* and was no doubt a great experimenter. It is said that he was one of the first scientists to dissect animals. Yet he was also a believer in the philosopher's stone, although he thought that alchemy was more for magicians than for scientists.

However, he was always careful to explain that no one knows where magic leaves off and science begins. For example, he believed in the divining rod—a stick that is held in the hand and thought, by some, to twitch when the holder passes over an underground source of water. He believed that such metals as the lodestone and such jewels as the emerald and sapphire had magical powers. As a matter of fact, he claimed to have been present at an operation in which a growth on a human being was magically removed by a sapphire.

Albertus had a few other strange beliefs, too. The heart, eye, or brain of a lapwing or a black plover hung on a man's neck would improve his memory. The heart of a turtledove wrapped in a wolf's skin would banish sexual desire. The plant, verbena, would cure pimples and cuts, and make a woman able to bear children. Putting camel's blood on a man's head would make him grow taller. The heart and tongue of a porpoise, when thrown in the water, would attract fish. Eating the heart of a weasel gave man the power to foretell the future. Eating the heart of a fox gave humans the ability to understand the language of the birds and beasts. If a lodestone was placed under a married woman's pillow and she fell out of bed—she was unfaithful.

At the time, there was a mythical beast that was quite popular in Europe. It was the basilisk, and was a legendary cross between a rooster and a serpent. Albertus believed that if you could find a basilisk, burn him up, and collect the ashes from the fire, these ashes would keep spiders away. He also said that silver rubbed with the

Some people thought
the divining rod could
be used to find water.

Many alchemists—like Albertus Magnus—were
also in the priesthood
where they could receive a good education.

burned remains of this animal would take on the appearance and weight of gold. Where Albertus intended to find
a basilisk is not known.

One historian claims that Albertus Magnus actually
found the philosopher's stone. Others say that it was
passed to him by the Dominican fathers. At any rate, it
was said to have a natural marking on it in the shape of a
serpent. And when Albertus put it down on the ground
in the woods, snakes were drawn to it. If Albertus did
find the stone, he made the mistake of turning it over to
his pupil, Thomas Aquinas, who destroyed it. Thomas,
it is said, thought a device such as this was the work of
the devil.

One of the strangest stories about Albertus Magnus
concerns a robot that he had invented. This automaton
was said to have had the shape of a human and the ability

Thomas Aquinas

to talk. For some unknown reason Thomas Aquinas again entered the history records and destroyed Albertus's mechanical man because he could not stand the robot's ceaseless screeches and chattering. What about this man St. Thomas?

He certainly seemed to have a peculiar hatred for noise. His study opened out onto a great thoroughfare, where grooms were continually exercising their horses. The noise prevented him from concentrating on his work, so St. Thomas supposedly made a magical miniature brass horse and buried it two or three feet under the surface of the middle of the road. From that time on, no horse would set foot on the road, and Thomas was able to work in peace and quiet.

Thomas Aquinas was born in 1225 to noble parents in Aquino, Sicily. His mother and father became upset when he joined the Dominican order at the age of eighteen. Their big objection was that he had chosen an order in which he would have to beg for his food. They even had two of his brothers lock him up for two years. The brothers were said to have sent women into his cell to try and get St. Thomas to break his vow of celibacy. But it didn't work.

Finally, in 1245, Emperor Frederick II set him free. Thomas then went to Cologne and placed himself under the protection of Albertus Magnus. Later they ended up in Paris. There, Thomas was made an abbot. He was canonized only 49 years after his death.

But what has St. Thomas to do with alchemy? To begin, he was quite interested in natural history and the sciences, probably having picked up this interest from his tutor. Although he was a man of religion he also believed in magic. He thought there were such things as witches and demons and he was a follower of astrology. He believed that magicians had occult powers and that men could be made invisible. In addition he was sure that it was possible to create a homunculus—an artificial man. At any rate Thomas was a dabbler in the alchemic art and his reputation was almost as well-known as another magnificent scientist of the period, Roger Bacon.

Roger Bacon was a scientist through and through. He had very little patience with the scientist-priests, as Thomas Aquinas or Albertus Magnus were referred to. He called them the "holy-order boys, who enter the order before their twentieth birthday."

Bacon was born in England, in 1214, during a time when all scientific belief was based upon the opinions of the masters of the past, regardless of whether or not they were true. If Aristotle had said that a human being had 100 teeth, we could almost assume that the scientists of this time period would have believed it.

But the Franciscan friar, Roger Bacon, was a radical. He used his own methods to find out the truth by experimenting in his laboratory. Since he was living in an era when almost everybody believed in magic, you can imagine what a stir was caused when Bacon came out with his book, *Epistle on the Secret Workings of Art and Nature and the Nonsensicality of Magic.*

There were reasons for Bacon being a radical. Shortly after his birth, his parents were forced by the crown to take him and leave England. They had taken the wrong side in the Baron's War against King John. This war ultimately resulted in the signing of the Magna Carta in 1215.

We don't know where they hid, but the story goes that they had very little money, and Roger eventually had to earn a living by doing copywork for students, and writing grammar books in Latin, Greek, and Hebrew. Some believe he worked too hard and had a nervous breakdown as a result.

Even when he was quite young, Bacon showed a talent for science. He wrote a paper on perspective, and even explained why the sun and the moon appear to be larger when they are near the horizon. It is said that he invented a compound similar to gunpowder which would explode even under water. Supposedly he worked on navigational instruments and made a better compass.

And there are even theories which suggest that he invented eyeglasses and predicted the invention of the airplane.

But for all his scientific theories, Bacon, too, believed that base metals could be changed into gold. And he also tried to find the elixir of life and manufacture medicines which would prolong life.

Unfortunately, this rebel spent a total of 12 years in prison during his lifetime. Two different Popes sent him to jail. The first time occurred in 1264. Pope Urban IV denied Bacon the right to teach and then had him thrown into a cell. The sentence didn't last too long, since the Pope soon died. And, in 1265, Clement IV, the next Pope and a friend of Bacon's, let him out of prison. He had met the alchemist while he was on Vatican business in England, and later even invited him to the papal court.

Bacon went on teaching that science should be a part of the curriculum in the seminaries, and got into trouble again when Clement, his protector, died. The minister-general of the Franciscan Order, who later became Pope Nicholas IV, had him thrown into jail once more. This time he stayed there for ten years, until Nicholas died in 1294. Bacon lived only a few months after the Pope's death.

The first alchemist who recorded his experiments was Arnaldo Bachuone, known to us as Arnold de Villanova.

He was born in Villanova, Spain, in 1235, and was trained in a Dominican monastery.

After his education, he settled in Barcelona, opened his doctor's office and began to write books. These books were about medicine (health rules, cures, antidotes, and special texts on epilepsy, gallstones, and gout) and magic and astrology. Some feel that he was a rather superstitious man, since he believed diseases were influenced by the planets. Astrology was used in his treatments, along with spoken spells and magic jewelry.

Arnold, too, was a fan of the emerald. He told his king to hang an emerald necklace around the necks of newborn infants in order to prevent epilepsy. He also used other stones, plants, and animal substances for his cures. A coral chain touching the abdomen would prevent stomach-aches. For sore feet, frogs' legs, eagle talons, turtle feet, or a lodestone could be tied to the patient's own feet. If an insane person had a cross-shaped incision cut in his scalp, the harmful vapors of insanity would supposedly escape from his head.

Arnold believed in the philosopher's stone. And at least one person claimed to have seen Arnold change base metals into gold. He was a professor of theology named Johannes Andreae. He wrote, "During our time there was also present at the papal court one Arnold of Villanova, who is an authority in the fields of theology and medicine. He is a great alchemist also and left for all of us to meditate upon some golden scepters which he made."

Eventually, Arnold found himself in a lot of trouble. In 1285 King Peter III of Aragon was dangerously ill, and he summoned the physician. It is said that Arnold prophesied that the king would die within the year, which came to pass. In the meantime, the alchemist had forecast that the world would come to an end in 1335, which did not come to pass. You win a few and you lose a few. But these predictions, and many others, began to cause the Pope to become suspicious of Arnold's powers.

Arnold kept on antagonizing the authorities. He stated that papal edicts were merely works of man rather than of God. He said that being charitable toward others was more important than going to weekly mass. In 1299 the Archbishop of Tarragona excommunicated him. Arnold escaped to Paris, but was captured by the Inquisition, where he was tried and convicted of working with the devil. He apologized, and, surprisingly enough, the church court let him leave France.

He went to Genoa and began to practice again. He sent a copy of his latest book to Pope Boniface with the idea that the Pope would be pleased. Not so. Boniface declared that the book should have been submitted to the papacy before publication, and threw the poor alchemist in jail. The Inquisition banned all of his writings.

Then came another trial before the church authorities. Arnold was forced to recant again, and this time he was condemned to be burned at the stake. But, like the ending of an old movie where the cavalry arrives at the last minute, the Pope became ill and Arnold cured him—perhaps with one of his magic charms.

Later, he was appointed court physician, with a private castle thrown in. He died in 1310 in a shipwreck during one of his many journeys.

Another Spanish alchemist was born on the Island of Majorca in the Mediterranean Sea off the coast of Spain in 1235. Raymond Lull (or Lully) was the son of the governor of the island, and it seems that he was not much more than a playboy until he had reached the age of 30. He started out as a page to the king and eventually became Master of the Palace.

But even after he was married and the father of two boys and a girl, he was still chasing the ladies. On one occasion, it is said, he was riding a horse and decided to chase a lady through the streets. She ran into the cathedral, and Lull followed her in, horse and all.

Because the girl was married, Lull apologized by writing her a love sonnet. She and her husband, being kindly souls, realized that the only way to discourage Raymond was to tell him the truth—she was suffering from incurable cancer. Lull was so filled with remorse that he gave away all of his money, switched to a religious life, and promised to serve God.

It is said that Lull was a student of Arnold de Villanova although there is disagreement about this. At any rate, he became a Franciscan friar and began to study Arabic in order to become a missionary to the Arabs. While learning the language, he also became interested in Arabian philosophy and alchemy.

He then set out on his pilgrimage to the Arabs. A story is told of Lull's kindness. It seems that he had hired a young Arab as his valet and language teacher. But when the young man found out that Lull intended to preach against Mohammedanism, he stabbed his master in the chest. Lull, wounded and bleeding, forgave him and even attempted to prevent the police from putting the servant in jail. But the Arab was sent to prison, where he hanged himself in frustration.

Lull, because of his alchemic studies, began to take the idea of changing mercury into gold very seriously. It is said that he once remarked: "Were there enough mercury, I could transform whole oceans into gold."

All that he needed, he thought, was a piece of the philosopher's stone the size of a bean, and he could change 1000 ounces of mercury into a red powder. Then this red powder could be used as a philosopher's stone of great power. Next he would take one ounce of this powder and change another thousand ounces of mercury into more red powder. When he could do this one more time, the power of the red powder would be so strong that gold would be the result of the transformation. Unfortunately, he never found his bean-sized piece of stone.

In 1291 he was again in Arabia and was condemned to death by the King of Tunis, but the sentence was set aside by this ruler and exile was substituted. In 1308 in Algiers he was so successful in converting people to Christianity that the authorities tried to stop his preaching. He was sentenced to wear a tight horse bridle, a bit was put into his mouth, and he was not permitted to speak. After forty days of this, he was publically beaten and thrown out of town.

Knowing that he was under a death sentence if he ignored his exile orders, Lull courageously returned to Tunis. Soon afterwards he was stoned to death.

Shortly after Lull's time, alchemists, in addition to searching for methods of turning base metals into gold, became even more concerned in looking for the elixir of life. Power, they probably felt, belonged to the one who could prolong life.

The Fountain of Youth

♄

FIVE / THE FOUNTAIN OF YOUTH / It probably has occurred to all of us at one time or another that it might be nice to live forever. And the alchemists were no exception. So, early in the game, they began to search for the elixir of life—that elusive material that would keep all people young forever.

The elixir of life was at first thought to be a magical substance which could prolong life, cure diseases, or turn base metals into gold. But as time went on, the alchemists began to believe that the elixir was to be used in preventing sickness and lengthening life. The philosopher's stone, they felt, would take care of changing metal to gold.

During this period of history, it was believed that all diseases were caused by an imbalance of the elements of the human body. So the elixir was merely a cure to straighten out this imbalance. One of the recipes for this substance was outlined by a seventeenth century French alchemist.

"Take three parts of red earth (the philosopher's stone, which no one could find), water and air, six parts altogether, mix them thoroughly and prepare a metallic paste like butter in which the earth can no longer be felt with the finger. Add one and a half parts of fire and place it into a thoroughly closed vessel and give it fire of the first degree for digestion. Then you prepare an extract of the elements according to the degrees of the fire until they are reduced to a solid earth. The matter becomes like a shining, translucent red stone and then it is ready. Put it into a pot on a modest fire and moisten it by its oil, drop by drop, until it becomes fluent without smoke. Do not be afraid that the mercury will vaporize; the earth drinks the humidity eagerly, because it is a part of its nature. Now you have the elixir ready. Thank God for his grace that he has granted you, use it for his praise and keep the secret."

Another early formula for the elixir suggested that one must mix eight pounds of sugar of mercury with a piece of the philosopher's stone. Then add calomel, gentian, cinnamon, aniseed, nard, coral, tartar, and mace. The trouble occurred, of course, when the ingredients had to be found in order to be used. It then said to drink this brew mixed with wine or bromium, night and morning during the first month. Then switch to the morning only in the second month, and then take it three times per week for the rest of one's life. (Who wants to live forever?)

But for the recipe written in real alchemic language, consider this suggestion:

"Ten parts of coelestiall slime; separate the male from the female, and each afterwards from its own earth, physically, mark you, and with no violence. Conjoin after separation in due, harmonic vitall proportion; and straightway, the Soul descending from the pyroplastic sphere, shall restore, by a mirific embrace, its dead and deserted body. Proceed according to the Volcanico magica theory, till they are exalted into the Fifth Metaphysical Rota. This is that world-renowned medicine, whereof so many have scribbled, which, notwithstanding, so few have known."

What do you suppose that meant?

The man who has the honor of being the first person to gain a reputation for experimenting on himself was Nicolas Flamel. He was a Frenchman who tried to make the elixir of life and then swallowed it. Since he was born in 1330 and lived only until 1417 or 1418, it would seem that he had the wrong formula. After all, a life of 87 or 88 years is not forever.

One of the most widely traveled of all the alchemists was Heinrich Cornelius Agrippa. But not all of his moves

Nicolas Flamel

from place to place were caused by his desire to see the world. Sometimes he was merely thrown out of the country where he was living.

Agrippa was born in Cologne, Germany in 1486 and apparently was given a fine education for the times. He claimed that he could speak eight languages, and boasted that in six of them he was able "not only to speak them," but express himself "elegantly in them and dictate in and translate them." He was also a student of both the law and the occult sciences.

When word got out that Heinrich was able to make gold, he was hired by the Emperor Maximilian as a sort of combination alchemist and diplomatic courier. So, at the age of 21, Agrippa found himself sent on a secret mission. His job was to try to get the King of France to join forces with Maximilian in order to invade Venice.

We do not know if he was successful in this mission, but we do know that while he was in France he started a secret society to study magic, alchemy, and astrology. But it seems that the people of the society had other interests, too. One of the members was a young Spaniard whose castle had been seized by peasants. Agrippa and his friends decided to try to recapture it for their friend.

The members of the society got into the castle but the peasants brought up reinforcements and surrounded them. Young Heinrich was barely able to escape with his life.

After this disaster he must have been afraid to go home since he wandered around Spain and Italy. Eventually he landed a job in 1509 at Dole University in France. Once again Agrippa got into trouble. He began to lecture against the beliefs of a powerful university professor—a specialist in the art of numerology (foretelling the future with numbers). The professor was very influential with the crown at the time and Heinrich was able to avoid arrest only by running off to England.

He stayed there for a year but then traveled to Cologne and finally to Würzburg where he met an abbot who was a skilled alchemist. Heinrich became interested in this man's work and wrote a book called *De Occulta Philosophia*. When the book was published, Agrippa was only 24. He was a man of much fame and some fairly strange ideas.

He wrote of certain plants that could bring the dead back to life, love potions, and the idea that a pregnant woman's experiences could mark her unborn child in some way or other. He also believed that the letters of the alphabet had mysterious powers, and related them to the signs of the zodiac.

After his book was published, Agrippa was appointed as an imperial counselor by the Emperor Maximilian, went off to battle, and was so brave that he was made a knight. But his patience was still in short supply and he wandered off again—this time to Italy. For the next several years Agrippa journeyed to many cities all over Europe. He was thrown out of one city when he tried to defend an accused witch, and he made an enemy of the Queen of France when he refused to prophesy the outcome of a current war.

Even in the Netherlands his job as royal court registrar lasted for only two years. Agrippa was accused of witchcraft and thrown into a jail in Brussels. His enemies stated that he was in league with the devil. And a black dog, which was actually his pet, was really Satan in disguise.

Upon his release from prison, Agrippa turned his back on his belief in alchemy and wrote the following:

"What madness then, when after all the money, time, and effort is expended, they expect gold, youth, and immor-

Kaÿser Rudolphus der Ander

Did Emperor Rudolph II
protect alchemists out of his human kindness?
Or scientific curiosity?
Or greed?

tality in return. In the end they finish by being old, in rags, emaciated, and crippled by mercurial poisoning. They are rich only in need and are so poor they would sell their soul for a farthing in a trice. Thus they have achieved in themselves the transmutation they would have fain worked in the metals, for, instead of alchemists, they are pseudochemists, instead of doctors, beggars, the laughing-stock of the people."

Agrippa died in Grenoble, France, in 1535.

Frequently, alchemists acquired the interest of wealthy patrons who furnished laboratories and supported their experiments. One of the best friends the alchemists ever had was the Emperor Rudolph II of Austria. He had a peculiar habit of collecting alchemists. It was said that at one time or another there were more than 200 alchemists working for the emperor.

The laboratory, according to legend, was in a section of Prague, Czechoslovakia, known as Alchemists' Alley. One of the men working there, Michael Sendivoi (Sendivogius), was said to have created gold, and Rudolph was easily convinced this was so. Thus he had a marble plaque made which read "May everyone achieve what the Pole Sendivogius has wrought."

To tell Sendivogius's story, however, one must first go back and mention another alchemist, a Scotsman named Alexander Seton, who called himself Cosmopolites. As the story is told Cosmopolites discovered a way to convert a lump of lead into gold. And always in his travels he would give away this precious metal to those who were in need, keeping nothing for himself.

His secret, the legend is told, was a supply of red powder. And he never shared his formula with anyone. Well, this couldn't go on for long and greedy people began to hear of Cosmopolites' work. Finally, the King of Saxony (later a part of Germany) captured the alchemist and threw him in prison until he could make Cosmopolites give up his secrets.

But Cosmopolites kept silent. He was guarded night and day by forty soldiers, pierced with pointed iron bars, scorched with molten lead, burned by fire, beaten, and put on the rack. Yet he never told his formula.

Eventually, this man's plight reached the ears of Sendivogius, who was nearby. He asked if he might talk with Cosmopolites to learn his secrets. It's possible that the prisoner was becoming restless and sought a means of escape. So he told Sendivogius that he must pay for in gold anything that was revealed.

Lacking money, Sendivogius went to his home town of Krakow, Poland, sold his house, and returned to Dresden with some money. He began to see the captive in his cell every day and in the process became very friendly with the prison guards. One night he threw a party and got the guards drunk. He and Cosmopolites escaped.

They headed for Krakow, and when they reached it, Sendivogius presented his bill. The price for Cosmopolites' freedom was a copy of the recipe for his formula.

Cosmopolites refused to give up the recipe, but did promise to deliver one ounce of the red powder. Sendivogius took it, but Cosmopolites was so weakened by the torture that he died soon after. So Sendivogius decided that he would go back to Dresden and look through the dead man's property, hoping to find the formula.

But the widow was protecting the papers of her late husband. What could Sendivogius do but marry her? He never found the formula, but he still had the ounce of red powder. He had several demonstrations and con-

John Dee

vinced a few people he could turn metal into gold. Next he wrote a book concerning his experiments and it was from this volume that Emperor Rudolph II heard of him. This is certainly a very complicated way to get your name on a plaque.

It wasn't long before the news of Rudolph's interest in alchemy reached England. And soon after this the astrologer to Queen Elizabeth I, John Dee, and his assistant

Edward Kelley

Edward Kelley, both alchemists, visited Rudolph.

Dee did not practice much alchemy at the court, but seemed to content himself with making magic mirrors and foretelling the emperor's future by means of astrology. He and Rudolph became such good friends that jealous people at court started a rumor that he was going to murder the emperor. So Rudolph was forced to throw him out of the country.

EDW.D KELLY, A MAGICIAN.

in the Act of invoking the Spirit of a Desceased Person.

Sibly Del.   Ames Sculp.

D.r Dees Works

An eighteenth century engraving
of Edward Kelley and John Dee
as they raised the spirit of a dead woman

Kelley, however, stayed on. This may have been a bad mistake on his part. It is said that he made gold for the emperor and even developed an elixir of life. But the court was still full of envious people. So a fight was engineered between Kelley and a young nobleman. The alchemist stabbed the nobleman, but was arrested. When he tried to escape from jail, he accidentally broke his leg. As the legend is told, Kelley was returned to jail, where he was given no medical treatment. In time he died of a leg infection.

Rudolph, however, continued to help his alchemists. He told his Spanish ambassador to send people out to look for the so-called *bezoar stones.* These were supposed to be stones found in the stomachs of animals and were used to relieve melancholy and high blood pressure.

In 1612, Rudolph developed a case of gangrene. Even though he took a dose of a potion made from bezoar stones, he died in January of that year.

As we've seen, not too many of the practicing alchemists were strictly honest. Let's look at a few more of the rogues in this business.

SIX / THE SWINDLERS / One of the earliest fakes was Daniel von Siebenbürgen. He arrived in Florence, Italy and offered Cosimo I, the present ruler, a little diversion. Daniel claimed that he could take a common drug of the time, *usafur,* and turn it into gold. Now the catch was that usafur was not a drug at all. This charlatan was very cagey. So he sold a quantity of gold amalgam (part gold, but mostly mercury) to every medical shop in the city and called the amalgam usafur.

Then he told Cosimo to send a messenger to any drug store in the city to bring back a portion of this medicine. When a bit of the drug was brought back, it was easy enough for him to turn it into gold by heating it and removing the melted precious metal.

Cosimo was thrilled. He wanted more and more gold. But the apothecary shops of Florence suddenly ran out of usafur. So what did our brave alchemist do then? He got 20,000 ducats from Cosimo on the pretext of going to France to find more of the magic substance. It is not surprising that Daniel was never seen in Florence again.

Duke Julius of Brunswick-Wolfenbüttel was the victim of a huge conspiracy. Near the end of the sixteenth century, a former clergyman, Philipp Soemmering, went into partnership with another man of the cloth, Abel Scherding. They faked a transmutation of gold for King Johann Friedrich II of Germany. Their reward was eight ounces of gold and 760 talers. The two suddenly rich men ran off to Brunswick before their dishonesty was discovered.

In Brunswick, Soemmering picked up another partner, a court jester whose nickname translated into something like Harry the Squint. He brought his girl friend along, Anne Marie. She eventually became the boss of the operation. She hired one more member to join the syndicate, Sylvester Schulfermann, and they all trooped off to see the local duke.

They claimed that they could increase the output of the Brunswick salt mines. Furthermore, after they had done this, they said they would give a magic stone to the duke enabling him to do the same thing. Next they persuaded the duke to advance them 2000 talers and appoint Soemmering as head of the laboratory.

There is some evidence that Soemmering believed Anne Marie could work magic. But Schulfermann was

A woodcut showing
a sixteenth century mine

not fooled by her and began to doubt the entire escapade. So he left the group and picked up another partner, a man named Kettwig.

However, it wasn't long before Soemmering discovered Anne Marie was as much a fake as any of them and he too began to get cold feet. So for some strange reason, he went to the duke and asked that he, Anne Marie, and Harry the Squint be fired.

The duke deported Anne Marie and Harry, but ordered Soemmering to stay on and complete the bargain that he had made—that of building up the salt output.

What could Soemmering do but try to get away? He was caught, however, as were all the rest of the tribe. And their plot was discovered. After a bit of torture, the trial began. Justice was swift. Soemmering and Harry were torn to pieces with red hot tongs, then dragged and quartered. Anne Marie was pinched with tongs and

burned to death in an iron chair. Schulfermann and Kettwig were dragged behind horses, broken on the wheel, and finally quartered. Whatever pieces of their bodies could be found were hung on gallows. It is not surprising that the duke then outlawed all alchemists in Brunswick. Needless to say, alchemists steered clear of the duke.

One of the great fakes of all time was Joseph-François Borri, who was born in Milan in 1627. Because he was always in trouble with the police, he continually asked for sanctuary in the church to protect himself from the people that he had wronged.

Next he pretended that God had spoken to him and told him that it was his special mission to reform mankind.

He claimed to wear a wondrous sword which St. Michael had given him, and he said that a miraculous palm-branch was being reserved in his name in heaven.

Most of this was accepted by the people in the town. But Borri went too far when he claimed that he was the incarnation of the Holy Spirit. The townspeople and clergy had had enough. Borri was condemned to death by the Inquisition for heresy.

Somehow he managed to escape his execution and went to Germany. There he was able to convince Queen Christina that he could manufacture the philosopher's stone. Of course he never could and was soon exposed as a fake. But once again before any punishment could be enacted he escaped to Denmark and tried to sail to Turkey. However, he was found by the police and sent back to Rome, where he died in prison in 1695.

Johann Friedrich Böttger was born in Magdeburg, Germany, in 1685. At the age of 12 he was apprenticed to an apothecary in Berlin and studied alchemy. Sometimes he stayed up all night doing experiments with various chemicals that he had stolen from his tutor. One morning he was so sleepy that he made many mistakes as he filled prescriptions. When someone handed him a bottle of red liquid Johann applied a small amount of this to some mercury. The result was a substance which resembled gold. Suddenly Johann was in another business entirely, that of manufacturing gold. Shortly afterwards, he ran away from his master and began living the high life in the city. When his money ran out Johann returned to his laboratory, tried a few more experiments, and then declared that once again he had transformed metal into gold. Success came quickly to the young man, and finally even King Frederick I heard about him.

Frederick ran a very expensive court and needed an alchemist to furnish him with gold. When Böttger heard that the king wanted to see him, he did a very smart thing —he escaped from Berlin to Saxony. Obviously he was afraid of being exposed as a fake.

Alchemists and workers
are busy changing base metals
into gold. Two unidentified
alchemists appear to be checking
the formula.

The king, however, offered a reward for Johann and sent a troop of soldiers after him. But the captain of the soldiers in Saxony was just as greedy as the King. When he heard why Johann was wanted, he substituted another man in place of Böttger and turned the imposter over to the Berlin constabulary.

Unfortunately for Johann, Augustus, the ruler of Saxony, needed money as much as Frederick. So he "protected" his new-found alchemist and refused to send him back to Berlin. As a matter of fact, Böttger was taken to Dresden and kept safely in a large house, guarded by soldiers. While he was there, he was encouraged to use his laboratory. He was safe, or so he thought.

Böttger learned how safe he was. To begin, he was locked up with two guards at all times. Later he was transferred to the fortress of Königstein, where no one was permitted to see him. Of course the guards were nice to the 16 year old alchemist, and provided him with wine and beer every day. Kind as they were, Johann tried to commit suicide a few times during his imprisonment, but his guards prevented him.

Apparently, Augustus had a change of heart, for he brought Johann back to Dresden and set him up in another house—this time without so much security. Johann was still expected to produce gold and so he had to escape his golden cage. On his first try he was captured. Then Augustus began to get a little impatient, and demanded that Johann produce.

The young alchemist must have been a bright teen-ager. He asked that Augustus join him in a solemn oath. They both agreed that none of the proceeds of the gold-making would be used for "luxury, sinful living, malicious splurgings, unnecessary and unjust wars, and any such sinful deeds." Both of them took this oath. Johann apparently knew his man. The king would certainly spend some of the gold on these pursuits. And if one of the people involved in an alchemic oath breaks his word, no more gold can be made.

The trick worked. Many other oaths were sworn, but each time, no gold was made.

Although Augustus loved gold, he must have loved porcelain almost as much. Johann was still working in his laboratory when he discovered how to make a very superior porcelain. The king was almost as happy about this as he was about gold. So, Böttger decided to make a confession.

He admitted that he didn't have the least idea how to make gold. He was counting on the king's happiness with the new porcelain, and he fell on the mercy of the throne. Böttger asked to be sentenced to death. His luck held. Augustus set him free, but made him promise that he would never reveal the secret of the porcelain.

There are some people who just can't be trusted. The very next year, 1715, Johann sold the secret to the court physician in Berlin. In spite of this, Augustus gave him the right to manufacture the porcelain for as long as he was to live. Böttger was a rich man. And he set out to try to spend as much money as he could. He led a completely dissipated life, went blind, and died in 1719 at the age of 34 heavily in debt.

Very few records exist of the early days of our next faker. But it seems that he was the son of a poor peasant farmer who lived near Naples. One day he left the farm, renamed himself Don Domenico Manuel Caetano, Conte de Ruggiero, and went off to seek his fortune.

By 1695 it would have seemed that he indeed had found his fortune. At least he had found a vast treasure of alchemic recipes. There were those who said that he did not dig up this buried treasure with a shovel, but rather with a knife held at the throat of some unfortunate alchemist.

Anyway, he went to Madrid and was a sensation in the court of Spain. There he met an ambassador from Bavaria who was also a very good friend of the King. Naturally when the king heard about Domenico's abilities, he was very impressed and asked the alchemist to pay his court in Bavaria a visit. Domenico accepted and after a while was said to have produced a small quantity of gold. Maximilian, the king, was overjoyed, and soon Domenico was appointed General of Ordnance, Field Marshal, and even Honorary Commandant of the city of Munich.

For three years everyone was happy. But then the king began to notice that the count had not made any gold for awhile. Maximilian began to get restless. So he threw Domenico into jail for six years. No one knows how he escaped but he next appeared in Vienna, at the court of Emperor Leopold I. Domenico worked in the great alchemic laboratory there until the death of Leopold. Then he went to Berlin and was eventually murdered by an unknown enemy who was, perhaps, either jealous, greedy, or maybe both.

By now it may seem that all of the alchemists of the last few centuries were frauds. But that is not so. A few of them were honestly searching for the truth.

This alchemic illustration symbolizes the fertility
of the earth (represented by woman),
air (the man with the bellows at the right), fire (the sun at the left),
and water (cloud near the woman's shoulder).
The lion is an age-old symbol of protection,
and the figure of cupid stands for love.

SEVEN / MEN OF GOOD INTENTIONS /

While all of the frauds were in action, there was still a group of alchemists who were looking for ways to help mankind. The fakers had turned their backs on the true nature of alchemy, but the honest scientists were still carrying on the search for the philosopher's stone and the elixir of life. And most of them were preparing the way for modern chemistry and biology.

One of the most impressive alchemists of the time was Johann Baptist van Helmont, a Belgian scientist who was born to a noble family in 1577. He started studying mathematics but was so brilliant that by the time he was 17 he had become a physics lecturer at the university. And at the age of 22 he had obtained his medical degree. Then he discovered the teachings of Paracelsus.

The whole idea of chemical medicine so fascinated him that he retired to his castle near Brussels and spent the rest of his life experimenting in his laboratory. Even though he was invited by the Emperor to join the royal court as a chemist, he preferred to work in his laboratory. Johann ventured out to treat the sick, however, but never accepted fees. He died in his castle in 1624.

Van Helmont believed in the philosopher's stone, and even claimed to have made gold from mercury. He thought that all diseases were caused by *seeds*. These seeds, when mixed with water, would bring on an affliction. It is said that he had a mysterious stone, kept in oil or milk, which cured all kinds of diseases. Life was governed by a certain power which he called the *archeus*. And he believed in a substance he called the *enzyme*, which he said was the prime force of all body functions. Van Helmont was not too far off, either. From what we know of hormones today, we could guess that he had a slight knowledge of how the human glands worked.

It was during the seventeenth century, however, that alchemy began to give way to chemistry. And the guiding light of this transformation may well have been Robert Boyle. He was either the last of the great alchemists or the first of the great chemists.

Boyle was the younger son of the first Earl of Cork and was born in Lismore, Ireland, in 1627. He dedicated his life to the study of science, which was then called natural philosophy.

Virtue delt. & Sculp. 1739.   In the Collection of Dr. Mead. Impensis J. & P. Knapton Londini 1740.   J. Kesboom pinx.

Modern chemists claim Robert Boyle among their ranks, but few of them would include his belief in magic charms among modern techniques.

Boyle began his experiments at his estate, Stallbridge, in Ireland, moved to Oxford, and then to London. He was the first to point out that burning can only happen in the presence of air. He thought that air, therefore, must contain a living substance. It was Boyle who set chemistry on its experimental feet.

He had his blind side, too, of course. He believed that magic charms, when worn around the neck, would stop bleeding. Cramps could be eased by wearing a hippopotamus tooth, or a ring made of the hoof of an elk. There were certain metals that could be used either to cure children who had been hexed by a witch or to cure sufferers from hemorrhoids.

On the other hand, he was probably the first scientist to disprove Aristotle's theory that hot water freezes faster than cold water. He poo-poohed the use of divining rods to find water. He was also one of the first people to check the results of other scientists' work. Remember that today this is one of the most important parts of a science report—a new theory of discovery must be capable of being repeated by other scientists.

During his lifetime, Boyle described 301 medical experiments and invented 90 different medicines. When he died in London in 1691, science had turned the corner from alchemy to chemistry.

Are there modern alchemists? There certainly are. Let us take the case of one of them, Paul Mikhailoff, a modern English alchemist. During the day, he works in the Bank of England.

His grandfather, he claims, was an alchemist in Russia. His father fled to England, and Paul was told many stories about his grandfather's hobby. While he was in school, Paul did well in chemistry. Now he reads anything from nuclear physics to old alchemical works "in an attempt to get at the basic secret underlying the efforts of such master alchemists as Paracelsus and Alexander Seton." He does not believe in the spiritual side of alchemy, that is, the search to improve the human soul. He is content to hunt for the philosopher's stone and the elixir of life.

Paul tells of his work in this way: "By experimenting with chemistry and physics, I hope to provide a definite link between our world and the old civilization. There are lots of unexplained links . . . I'm sure that the old alchemists had a very vague inkling of what they were doing, and by repeating their experiments over and over again someday I shall arrive at a conclusion. I shall detect a clue, I'm certain, that will lead me to the transmutation point, the philosopher's stone, the truth. Call it what you like."

Perhaps he may.

Exact proportions of base metals
had to be measured before melting them.
But alchemists still had problems
in making gold.

EIGHT / SCIENCE AND ALCHEMY / Ignoring the quacks, frauds, and crackpots, we could say, by and large, that these alchemists were true scientists. They weren't all weird old men sitting around wearing high pointed hats and stirring up newts' feet and rattlesnakes' tongues in a cauldron. After all, Webster says that science is "knowledge obtained by study and practice!" Most of the people that we have met in this book are able to qualify.

Quite apart from their search for the philosopher's stone and the elixir of life, they discovered chemicals that we use in dyes, varnish, medicine, glass, and steel. They found cures for certain venereal diseases, and other ailments. They developed waterproofing for leather and cloth, rust inhibitors, luminous ink, smelling salts, sleeping potions, new kinds of explosives, and a drug that would combat pain. They were also the first to prepare

117

ammonium chloride, white lead, nitric acid, acetic acid and hundreds of other discoveries both chemical and medical.

As far as basic scientific understanding goes, one of these men developed the gas theory. Another was the first to think about the circulation of the blood, and still another started us on the road to the discoveries of the enzyme and the hormone. Many alchemists attempted to give an order to the elements—an attempt that culminated with the Periodic Table of the Elements as developed by Mendeleyev. Various other alchemic processes were helpful in establishing a way to manufacture the elements germanium and silicone which could be used in transistors. Your portable radios would weigh a lot more than they do now, and they would be many times more bulky, if we didn't have these substances.

What about their "crazy" ideas? Take one—the homunculus. It might seem silly to think that a little man could be grown in a bottle.

On the other hand, think of the teams of biologists who are right now working on ways to create life in a test tube. It may be possible to grow your own microbes by starting from scratch. And who knows? Some day we may have the secret of human life.

What about that insane search for the philosopher's stone? Well, we now know that many substances can change into others. For example, over a period of many many years, radioactive radium will eventually turn into lead. Might that not be called reverse transmutation? And in 1970, a team of scientists at the University of California created another new element and suggested that it be called Hahnium. This element had never existed before, and the scientists had manufactured it by bombarding another man-made element, Californium, with nitrogen ions. They had changed one element into another. Isn't that what our old friends, the alchemists, were trying to do?

How about that crazy elixir of life? Think for a minute. Isn't that what most medical researchers are still looking for? Was Salk crazy when he developed the polio vaccine? Was Fleming crazy when he discovered penicillin? No, and neither were the alchemists when they searched for the elixir of life.

Actually, the honest alchemist was only at fault for believing that he had discovered the philosopher's stone and that he had made gold in his laboratory. Many of these men, however, were engaged in the process of heating mercury. The vapors of this metal can produce hallucinations when inhaled. It's possible that many individuals were influenced by the fumes.

Then too, alchemists were not as sophisticated as are modern chemists. Perhaps any yellow-colored metal or

This woodcut represents the
transmutation, or changing, of the metals.
The king is the metal gold.

silver-colored metal would appear to be real gold or silver
to them. By accident they might have been able to change
the color of a base metal and then believed that they had
made gold or silver. Certain arsenic compounds when
combined with copper will change some metals to sil-
very-looking alloys. And copper itself, when mixed with
certain chemicals, can be part of a gold-looking alloy—
brass is an example of this.

All in all, we might well pay attention to the great
British chemist, Sir William Ramsey: ". . . the transmu-
tations of the elements no longer appears to be an idle
dream. The philosopher's stone will [be] discovered,
and it is not beyond the bounds of possibility that it
may lead to that other goal of the philosophers of the
dark ages—the *elixir vitae*. For the action of living cells
is also dependent on the nature and direction of the
energy which they contain; and who can say that it will
be impossible to control their action, when the means of
imparting and controlling energy shall have been
investigated?"

ACKNOWLEDGEMENTS

page 10: from an engraving by Wilhelm Koning, 1716

page 14: from *The Story of King Arthur and his Knights*, by Howard Pyle, New York, 1919

page 19: from a sixteenth century engraving, artist unknown

page 20: from the book, *Astronomica et Astrologica Opuscula*, Cologne, 1567

page 25: from the book, *Histoire de la Magic*, by Paul Christian, Paris, 1870

page 35: from a woodcut by Basile Valentin from *L'Azoth des Philosophes*, Paris, 1660

pages 38–39: by Ernst Lehner, from *The Picture Book of Symbols*, 1956

page 45: from the Austria National Library Picture Collection, artist unknown

page 48: from a seventeenth century woodcut, artist unknown

page 49: from a seventeenth century woodcut, artist unknown

page 52: from a seventeenth century engraving, Austria National Library Picture Collection, artist unknown

pages 56–57: from an old woodcut, artist unknown

page 60: from a seventeenth century woodcut, artist unknown

page 61: from the book, *Chymica: Basilica Philosophica*, by Mylius, Frankfurt, 1620

page 62: from a fourteenth century painting, Austria National Library Picture Collection, artist unknown page 65: from an eighteenth century engraving by de Bry

pages 68–69: from a woodcut by Georg Agricola, 1571

page 70: a painting from the Austria National Library Picture Collection, artist unknown

page 72: from an eighteenth century engraving, artist unknown

page 82: by Ernst Lehner, from *The Picture Book of Symbols*, 1956

page 86: from an eighteenth century engraving, artist unknown

page 90: from the Austria National Library Picture Collection, artist unknown

page 94: from an eighteenth century engraving, artist unknown

page 95: from an eighteenth century engraving, artist unknown

page 96: from an engraving by Sibly

page 101: from a woodcut by Sebastian Münster, 1544

pages 104–105: from a copperplate engraving by Johannes Stradanus, 1570

page 110: from a seventeenth century woodcut, artist unknown (portions of this woodcut are on pages 1–5)

page 113: from an engraving of 1739, artist unknown

page 116: from an old woodcut, artist unknown

page 120: from a seventeenth century woodcut, artist unknown

Chapter Symbols

Chapter symbols were taken from book *The Picture Book of Symbols*, William Penn Publishing Company, 1956. The artist is Ernst Lehner.

page 13: Chapter One, meaning mercury

page 33: Chapter Two, meaning gold

page 53: Chapter Three, meaning sulfur

page 64: Chapter Four, meaning brass

page 83: Chapter Five, meaning lead

page 98: Chapter Six, meaning silver

page 111: Chapter Seven, meaning copper

page 117: Chapter Eight, meaning nitric acid

INDEX

ABOUT THE AUTHOR / A curiosity for the unexplained and an infectious interest in the unknown—especially when writing about the supernatural—seem to be inherent qualities of the author.

Since earning his Ph.D. from Ohio State University, Thomas G. Aylesworth has been an assistant professor at Michigan State University and senior editor of Current Science. A senior editor for a New York City publishing firm, he and his family reside in Stamford, Connecticut.

Dr. Aylesworth is the author of eleven other intriguing and successful books. Among them are SERVANTS OF THE DEVIL, VAMPIRES AND OTHER GHOSTS, and WEREWOLVES AND OTHER MONSTERS.